UNUSUAL
ADVERTISING

monsa

UNUSUAL ADVERTISING

Copyright © 2014 Instituto Monsa de ediciones

Editor, concept, and project director
Josep María Minguet

Design and layout
Patricia Martínez (equipo editorial Monsa)

Translation
Babyl Traducciones

INSTITUTO MONSA DE EDICIONES
Gravina 43 (08930)
Sant Adrià de Besòs
Barcelona (Spain)
Tlf. +34 93 381 00 50
Fax.+34 93 381 00 93
www.monsa.com
monsa@monsa.com

Visit our official online store!
www.monsashop.com

Follow us on facebook!
facebook.com/monsashop

ISBN: 978-84-15829-63-8
D.L. B 11634-2014
Printed by Impuls 45

Photos:
All photographs for Monsa

Index

Advertising continues to evolve, we find works of art expressed in signs, magazines, or interacting with us.

In the following pages we will find some of the most impressive ads that have recently appeared,accompanied by the latest techniques in creativity. We have selected those campaigns that provoke a feeling in the viewer: They will make us laugh, think, enjoy....

The book is divided into three chapters: The first is dedicated to Guerilla Marketing. This concept refers to actions performed on the street, sometimes taking advantage of street furniture for the campaign (columns that become huge plants, road signs as lollipop...), and others performing giant models of the product, such as a marker, or taking advantage of something that already exists as a bowling pin, turning into teeth of a big mouth.

In the second chapter we will see the enormous possibilities of photography accompanied by a message, images that convey perfectly what the agencies wanted to show with that campaign, for example the use of the candle logo from Amnesty International, simulating burn the rope that is holding up the prisoners, or the advertising that promoted the vinyl records from "Fnac" company, using images of old glories of Rock, with the slogan "they will never die."

And in the third chapter we find the possibilities offered in illustration world, collage, photomontage,etc, to make campaigns in which the imagination plays an important role, like the one created for TMB in which they simulate different scenes from classic films such as King Kong, Godzilla or jaws, created by the Bassat Ogilvy agency.

"UNUSUAL ADVERTISING" brings together top creatives from the advertising industry.

Intro

La publicidad no deja de evolucionar: encontramos auténticas obras de arte plasmadas en carteles, revistas, o interactuando con nosotros por la calle.

En las siguientes páginas encontramos algunos de los anuncios más impactantes que han aparecido recientemente, acompañados de las últimas técnicas en creatividad. Hemos seleccionado aquellas campañas que provocan algún sentimiento en el espectador: nos harán reír, emocionarnos, pensar....

El libro se divide en tres capítulos: El primero está dedicado a la publicidad de Guerrilla. Este concepto se refiere a acciones realizadas en la calle, a veces aprovechando el mobiliario urbano como soporte del anuncio (columnas que se convierten en enormes plantas, señales de tráfico a modo de Chupa-chups...), y otras realizando maquetas gigantes del producto, como un rotulador, o aprovechando algo ya existente como los bolos de una bolera, que se convierten en dientes de una gran boca.

En el segundo capítulo observaremos las enormes posibilidades de la fotografía acompañados de un mensaje, imágenes que nos transmitirán a la perfección lo que han querido mostrar las agencias con esa campaña, como por ejemplo el uso del logotipo de la vela de Amnistía Internacional, simulando quemar la cuerda que retiene a unos presos, o el anuncio que promocionaba el Fnac de discos de vinilo, utilizando las imágenes de viejas glorias del Rock, con el eslogan "nunca morirán".

Y en el tercer capítulo encontramos las posibilidades que nos ofrece la ilustración, el collage, el fotomontaje, etc., para realizar campañas en las que la imaginación juega un papel importante, como la creada para TMB en la que simulan diferentes escenas de películas del cine clásico como King-Kong, Godzilla o Tiburón creadas por la agencia Bassat Ogilvy.

"UNUSUAL ADVERTISING" reúne a los mejores publicistas y creativos del mundo del marketing.

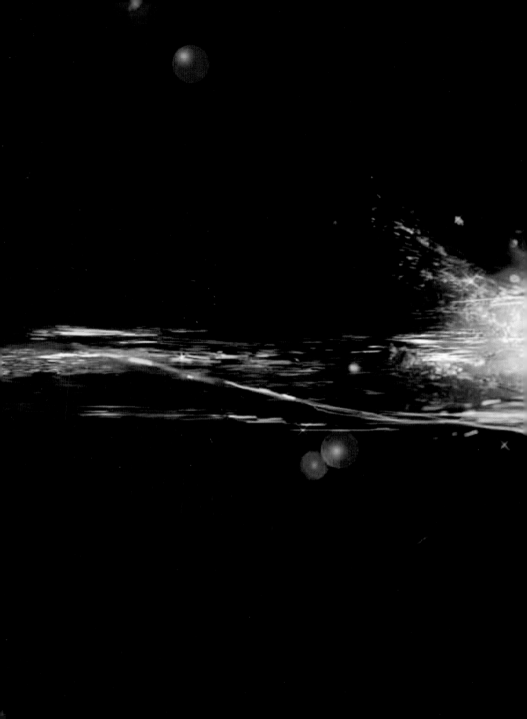

taste more

Guerrilla marketing

CHUPA-CHUPS: "GIANT LOLLIPOP"

School: European School of Design, Frankfurt, Germany
www.europeanschoolofdesign.eu
Creative Director: Ralph Thamm
Art Director / Photographer / Concept: Pavel Bondarenko
Copywriter: Reinhard Obinger

FEDEX KINKO: "GIANT WHITE-OUT" AND "GIANT HIGHLIGHTER"

Agency: BBDO, New York, USA
www.bbdo.com
Chief Creative Officer: David Lubars
Executive Creative Director: Eric Silver
Art Director: Chuck Tso
Copywriter: Eric Schutte

Get them off
your dog.

FRONTLINE
FLEA & TICK SPRAY
available at JAKPETZ

FRONTLINE: "MALL"

Agency: Saatchi & Saatchi Jakarta, Indonesia
www.saatchi.com
Chief Creative Officer: Andy Greenaway
Executive Creative Director: Juhi Kalia
Copywriters: Pancaputera, Juhi Kalia
Photographer: Heret Frasthio

IKEA: "STAIRCASE DRAWER"

Agency: Lowe & Partners, Kuala Lumpur, Malaysia
www.loweandpartners.com
Executive Creative Director: Ng Heok Seong
Creative Director: Ng Heok Seong
Copywriter: Mohan Prabhakar
Art Director: Joseph Lee
Illustrator: Desmond Phang

Ikea Japan: "Home Furnishing Liner"

Agency: ADK Tokyo, Japan / DRILL Tokyo, Japan
Executive Creative Director: Ken Shimizu
Creative Director: Osamu Enari
Copywriter: Takeshi Tsuji
Art Director: Akio Yamauchi

ENBW: "PLUG"

Agency: Jung von Matt/Elbe, Germany
www.jvm.com
Executive Creative Director: Wolf Heumann
Creative Directors: Sascha Hanke, Timm Hanebeck
Copywriter: Clemens Sehi
Art Director: Andy Tran
Graphics: Nadya Innamorato

MONDO PASTA: "NOODLESLURPER"

Agency: Jung von Matt/Hamburg, Germany
Creative Directors: Jan Rexhausen, Doerte Spengler-Ahrens
Art Director: Pablo Schencke
Copywriter: Sergio Penzo
Photographer: Uwe Huettner

MINI: "SIZE"

Agency: Jung von Matt/Zurich, Switzerland
www.jvm.com
Creative Directors: Michael Rottmann, Alexander Jaggy
Art Directors: David Hanselmann, Hendrik Schweder
Copywriters: Lars Haensell / Ole Kleinhans

SWEDISH ROYAL OPERA:
"ORPHEÉ"

Agency: Jung von Matt/Strömmen, Stockholm, Sweden
Art Directors: Max Larsson von Reybekiel, Jacob von Corswant
Copywriter: Magnus Andersson
Photographer: Sven Prim

KARSTADTQUELLE INSURANCE:
"BOWLING LANE"

Agency: Jung von Matt, Hamburg, Germany
Creative Directors: Deneke von Weltzien, Thimoteus Wagner, Fabian Frese
Account Directors: Anke Borchers, Jan Knauss
Copywriters: Thies Schuster, Max Biedermann

LAY'S: "POTATOES INSTALLATION"

Agency: Juniper Park
www.juniperpark.com
Creative directors: Terry Drummond and Alan Madill
Associate creative directors: Hylton Mann and Andy Linardatos
Client: Frito-Lay

HP ADVANCED PHOTO PAPER: "RIPPED"

Agency: Publicis Malaysia, MALAYSIA, Petaling Jaya
Executive creative director: Andy Soong
Art director: Andy Soong
Copywriter: Art Directors: Hong Xiao Yeen, Chong Khong Lum
Copywriters: Lisa Ng, Teh Le Vin, Ooi Toe Lee

SEMIRAMIS FERTILIZER: "PLANT PILLAR"

Agency: Scholz & Friends Hamburg
Creative direction: Tobias Holland
Art direction: Anna-Carina Thygs, Pedro Sydow
Text: Tina-Susan Rauter
Photography: Michael Dunlap
Picture editing: Dir Leisering

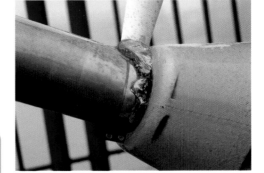

ALTECO SUPER GLUE: "STEEL SPAN WIRE"

Agency: DDB China Group Shanghai, China
Chief Creative Officer: Michael Dee
Creative director: Jody Xiong
Art directors: Jody Xiong, Jacky Xiao
Photography: Zhang Xin Hua
Copywriter: Jason Jin

DURACELL TORCHES: "AMBIENT LIGHTS"

Agency: Impact BBDO, Dubai, UAE
www.impactbbdo.com
Executive creative director: Oliver Maisey
Creative director: Jennie Morris
Art director: Mark Held
Illustrator: Mohsen Mahbob
Copywriter: Grant McGrath
Aditional credits: Media Hub

THERE'S NO BETTER MEDICINE FOR THE ENVIRONMENT THAN YOUR CONTRIBUTION

Why buy a laundry dryer, when you have the sun? You can put a clothes horse even in un-sunny seasons next to your bed and get dressed right from the line. By only doing this will you be saving 330 kilogram CO_2 for each person.

You can also save energy at the laundry itself: 40° Celsius on principle and without prewash is enough for 90% of all cases.

THIS IS HOW WE SAVE THE CLIMATE

THERE'S NO BETTER MEDICINE FOR THE ENVIRONMENT THAN YOUR CONTRIBUTION

Counteracting climate change can be so easy: For every casual 60W bulb, that's exchanged for a same bright 11W energy sufficient lamp and ran for around 700 hours, 20,5 kilogram CO_2 is saved.

That does not sound like very much, but if there's just one bulb per household swapped for a saving lamp, a whole (coal-fired) power plant can be shut off.

THIS IS HOW WE SAVE THE CLIMATE

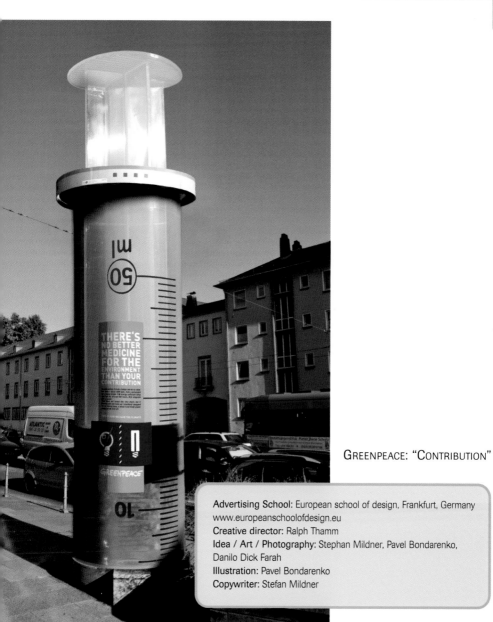

GREENPEACE: "CONTRIBUTION"

Advertising School: European school of design, Frankfurt, Germany
www.europeanschoolofdesign.eu
Creative director: Ralph Thamm
Idea / Art / Photography: Stephan Mildner, Pavel Bondarenko,
Danilo Dick Farah
Illustration: Pavel Bondarenko
Copywriter: Stefan Mildner

WWF: "Stop"

Agency: Saatchi & Saatchi Auckland, New Zeland
www.saatchiasiapacific.com
Executive creative director: Mike O'Sullivan
Creative director: Tim Hall
Art director: Ant Hatton
Copywriter: Robbie Brammall
Producer: Heath Davy

DEPARTMENT OF HEALTH / CANCER RESEARCH UK: "TANKER"

Agency: Ogilvy, London, UK
www.ogilvy.com
Executive Creative director: Malcolm Poynton
Creative director: Colin Nimick
Art director: Charlie Wilson
Copywriter: Emma de la Fosse

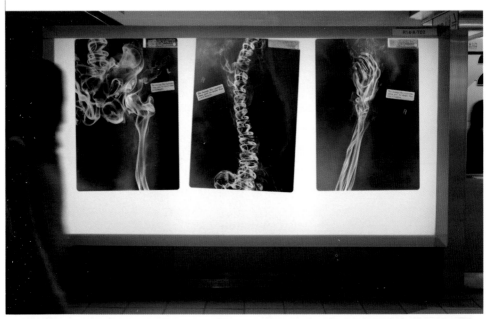

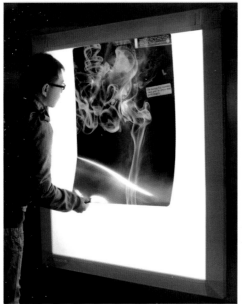

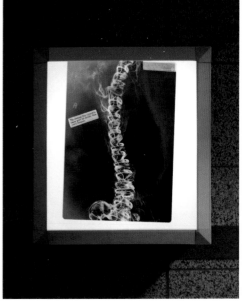

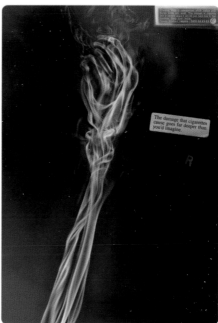

GOVERNMENT OF TAIWAN: "SMOKER'S HOTLINE"

Agency: Bates 141 Taiwan
www.bateschi.com
Executive creative director: Richard Yu
Creative director: Ronny Hsu, Lion Tsai
Copywriter: Lion Tsai, Renee Chen
Art director: Richard Yu, Ronny Hsu, Nelson Liu

FISH FRANKE: "FISH"

Agency: Publicis, Frankfurt, Germany
Chief creative officer: Stephan Ganser
Creative director (Art): Nico Juenger
Creative director (Copy): Peter Kaim
Account director: Sven Lohwasser
Photographer: Johannes Krzeslack
Architect: Thomas Breen

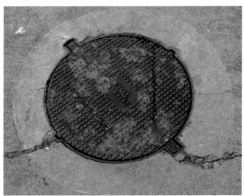

DUBLIN CITY COUNCIL: "PLUG PAVEMENT"

Agency: Publicis QMP, Dublin
www.publicis.ie
Creative director: Ger Roe
Art director: Ciaran McCarthy
Copywriter: Darragh Carey

TVNZ, TV2: "KILL BILL BLOOD SPLATTER"

Agency: Saatchi & Saatchi Auckland, New Zeland
www.saatchi.com
Executive creative director: Mike O'Sullivan
Art director: Matthew Swinburne
Copywriter: Helen Steemson
Producer: Anthony Martin

YOOJI'S RESTAURANT:
"SUSHI HAY-ROLLS"

Advertising agency: Jung Von Matt/Limmat
www.jvm.ch
Advertising campaign: giant sushi-california-rolls
Client: Yooji

1:00 pm

3:00 pm

5:00 pm

A specially designed awning placed above the board created a shadow that changed throughout the course of the day.

WWF: "Ocean levels"

Advertising agency: Draftfcb
www.draftfcb.com
Advertising campaign: Climate change
Client: World Wildlife Fund

Printed impact Ads

GET CAUGHT CARRYING AN ILLEGAL GUN
GET 3½ YEARS IN PRISON

CITIZENS CRIME COMMISSION OF NEW YORK CITY

CITIZENS CRIME COMMISSION: "GUNS = PRISON"

Advertising agency: Draftfcb
www.draftfcb.com
Client: Citizens Crime Commission of New York City

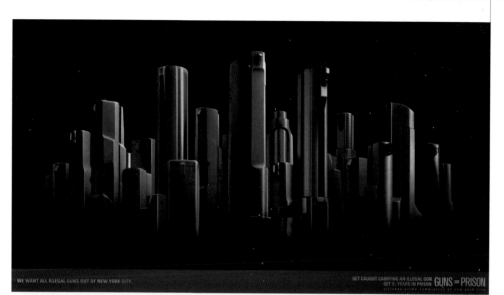

WE WANT ALL ILLEGAL GUNS OUT OF NEW YORK CITY.

GET CAUGHT CARRYING AN ILLEGAL GUN
GET 3½ YEARS IN PRISON GUNS = PRISON

PROTECTS WOOD

Ocedar: "Protects wood"

Advertising agency: Grey Group
www.grey.com
Client: Ocedar

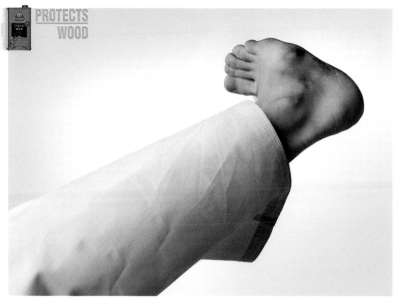

MICROAUDIO: "QUE TU OÍDO NO TE ALEJE"

Advertising agency: Kitchen
www.kitchen.es
Advertising campaign: Microaudio
Client: Multiópticas

Que
tu oído
no te
aleje

MicroAudio

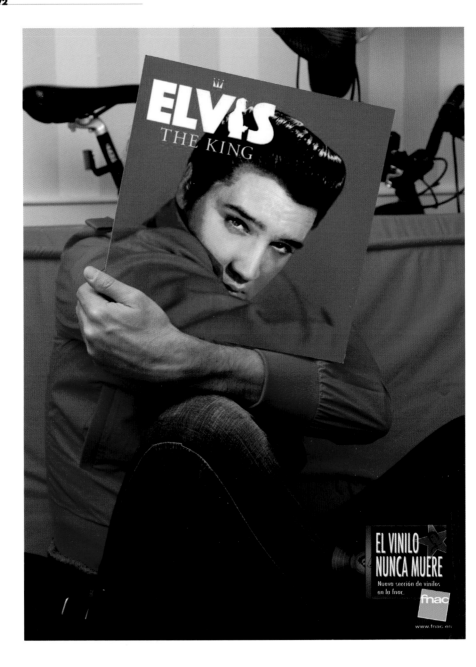

FNAC: "EL VINILO NUNCA MUERE"

Advertising agency: Kitchen
www.kitchen.es
Advertising campaign: New vinil section
Client: Fnac

AMNESTY INTERNATIONAL: "CANDLES"
"VELAS"

Advertising agency: Publicis Mojo
www.publicismojo.com
Advertising campaign: Candles
Client: Amnesty International

QUE NINGÚN PAÍS TORURE EN TU NOMBRE. Amnistía Internacional

QUE NINGÚN PAÍS TORURE EN TU NOMBRE. Amnistía Internacional

La pena de muerte es una práctica de otra época.
Todavía hay 76 países que la aplican.

Amnistía
Internacional

AMNESTY INTERNATIONAL: "BANDERAS"
"FLAGS"

Advertising agency: Contrapunto
www.contrapunto.es
Client: Amnistía Internacional

QUE NINGÚN PAÍS TORURE EN TU NOMBRE.

La pena de muerte es una práctica de otra época.
Todavía hay 76 países que la aplican.

Amnistía
Internacional

Bacardi: "Elixir"

Advertising agency: RKCR/Y&R
www.rkcryr.com
Client: Bacardi

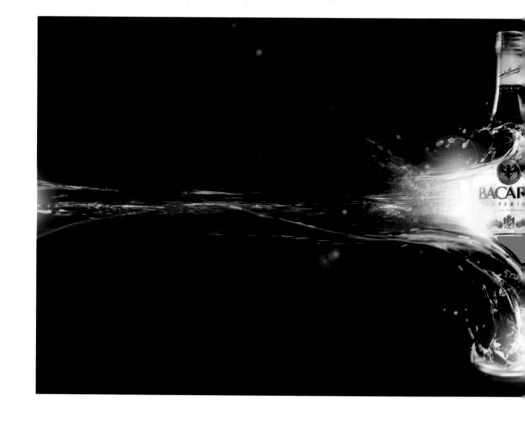

made to mix with cranberry taste more

taste more

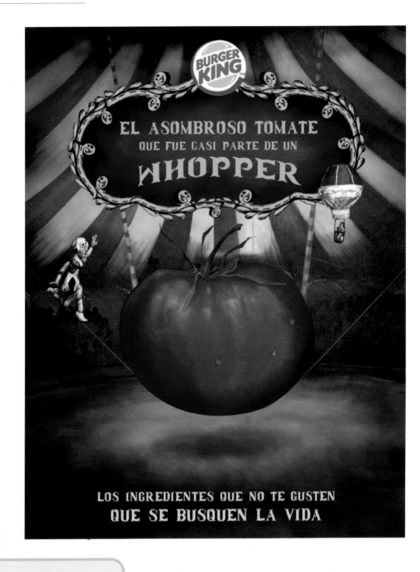

BURGER KING

Advertising agency: Zinkproject
Advertising campaign: Whopper
Client: Burger King

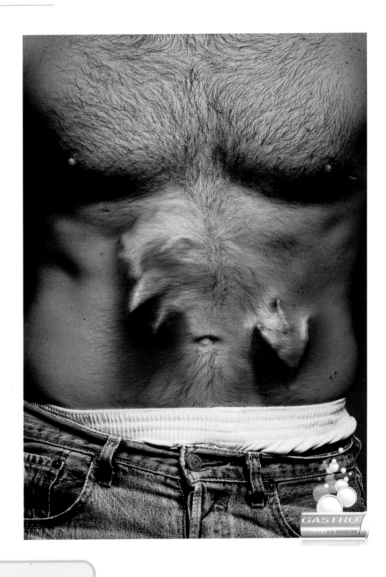

GASTRO:
"ACID INDIGESTION"

Advertising agency: Grey Group
www.grey.com
Client: Gastro

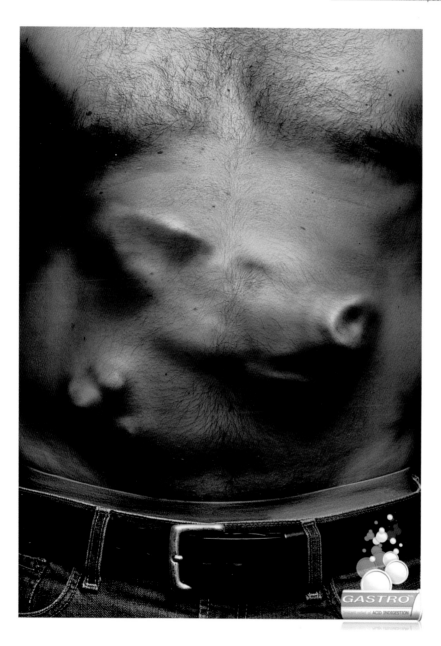

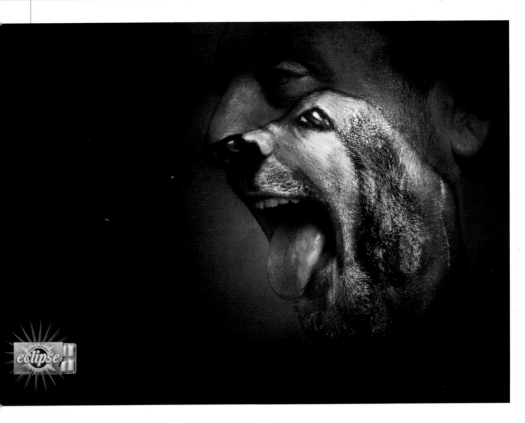

WRINGLEY ECLIPSE

Advertising agency: Tiempo BBDO
www.tiempobbdo.com
Client: Eclipse

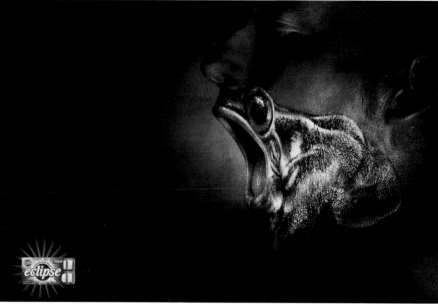

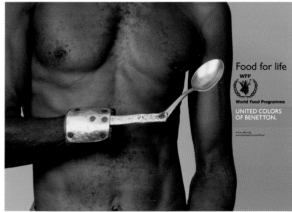

BENETTON

Advertising: Benetton
Advertising campaign: World Food Programme
www.benetton.com

Food
for work
Basmina, 15, is now free
to find work in Kabul.
Food aid supports her
while she looks for a job.

WFP
World Food Programme

UNITED COLORS
OF BENETTON.

Food
to go home
Argaleena, 9, and Mahjabina, 11,
return home from years
of exile in Pakistan.
Food aid supports their reset-
tlement and millions
of other Afghan refugees.

WFP
World Food Programme

UNITED COLORS
OF BENETTON.

SNICKERS: "MINI EXTREME"

Advertising agency: Tiempo BBDO
www.tiempobbdo.com
Client: Snickers

WORLD WILDLIFE FUND

Advertising agency: Draftfcb
www.draftfcb.com
Advertising campaign: Climate change
Client: World Wildlife Fund

WORLD WILDLIFE FUND

Advertising agency: Contrapunto
www.contrapunto.es
Advertising campaign: Contamination

BC LIONS

Agency: Rethink Advertising
www.rethinkcanada.com
Advertising campaign: BC Lions
Client: BC Lions

BC LIONS SEASON TICKETS 604 589-ROAR

BC LIONS SEASON TICKETS 604 589-ROAR

El 80% de las mujeres verá a una madre con un niño.
El 100% de los hombres no sabrá de qué niño hablamos.

CUESTIÓN DE SEXO | Todos los martes a las 22h00 | cuatro•

CADENA CUATRO

Agency: Kitchen
www.kitchen.es
Advertising campaign: Cuestión de sexo
Client: Cadena CUATRO

IF IT WAS THERE, IT'S HERE.

ROYAL **BC** MUSEUM

No *R.B.C.M. 977.188.1*   Artifact *Governess Trap*   Date *19th Century*

ROYAL BC MUSEUM

Agency: Rethink Advertising
www.rethinkcanada.com
Advertising campaign: Royal BC Museum
Client: Royal BC Museum

FRANCE 24

Advertising agency: Marcel Paris
www.marcelww.com
Advertising campaign: Beyond the news
Client: France 24

BEYOND THE NEWS

BEYOND THE NEWS

HOME OFFICE: "ENOUGH"

Advertising agency: RKCR/Y&R
www.rkcryr.com
Advertising campaign: Domestic Violence Reduction
Client: Home Office

Every week 2 women die
due to domestic violence.
Don't let your friend be 1 of them.

If you know your friend's being hit, it's time to put a stop to her abuse, before the abuser puts a stop to her. Help her take the first step; call the National Domestic Violence Helpline for support.

ENOUGH
0808 2000 247

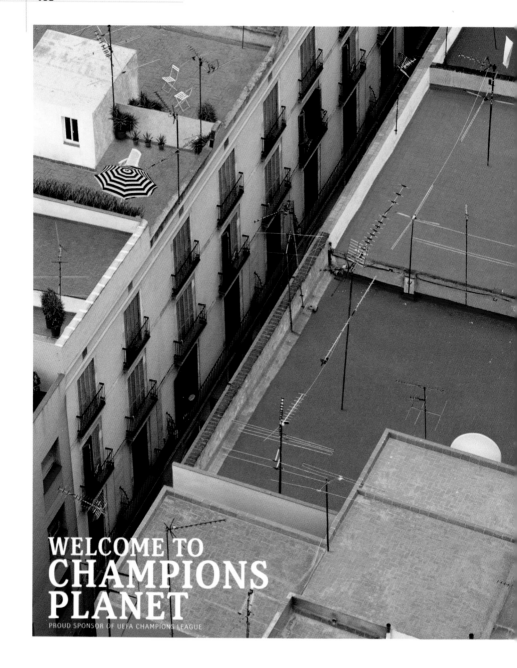

WELCOME TO
CHAMPIONS
PLANET
PROUD SPONSOR OF UEFA CHAMPIONS LEAGUE

HEINEKEN: "ROOFTOPS"

Agency: StrawberryFrog
www.rkcryr.com
Advertising
campaign: Champions League
Client: Heineken

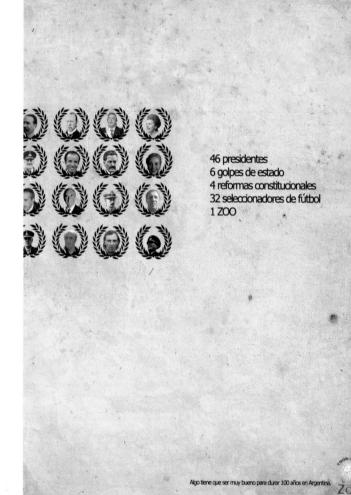

46 presidentes
6 golpes de estado
4 reformas constitucionales
32 seleccionadores de fútbol
1 ZOO

Algo tiene que ser muy bueno para durar 100 años en Argentina.

1906-2006

ZOO

ZOO BUENOS AIRES

Advertising agency: Zinkproject
Advertising campaign: Cambios
Client: Zoo Buenos Aires

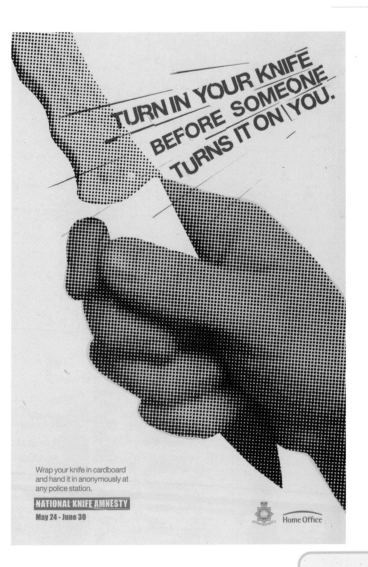

HOME OFFICE

Advertising agency: RKCR/Y&R
www.rkcryr.com
Advertising campaign: Knife Amnesty
Client: Home Office

WWF: "MONSTER"

Advertising agency: Zinkproject
Advertising campaign: Global Warming
Client: Adena (WWF Spain)

WWF: "Bomb"

Creative and exciting Ads

HAIR'S: "PAPER-HAIRDO"

Agency: Grey Beijing, China
www.grey.com
Art director: Shi Yuan He, Dan Fang, Chee Guan Yue
Executive creative director: Chee Guan Yue
Creative director: Dan Fang
Copywriter: Dong Hai Lui
Photographer: Edward Loh
Client: Hair's magazine

HAIR'S
THE MAGAZINE FOR SALON PROFESSIONALS

NOTHING
BUT THE HOTTEST
HAIRSTYLES

FAB DETERGENT: "ICE-CREAM" "KETCHUP" "SOUP"

Agency: Leo Burnett Company Inc.
www.leoburnett.com
Executive creative director: Chris Chiu
Creative director: Victor Ng, Jon Loke
Art director: Victor Ng, Jon Loke
Copywriter: Victor Ng, Jon Loke
Photographer: Xuan (Groovy Studios)
Client: Fab Detergent

PILOT: "GOLDFISHES"

Agency: Grey Beijing, China
www.grey.com
Executive creative director: Jürgen Krieger
Creative director: Jon Más, José Miguel Tortajada, Alex Martín
Art director: Dani Paez, Säul Serradesanferm, Oscar Amodia
Copywriter: Aitor Borras, Jorge Meneclier, Alberto Ramos
Client: Arge Pilot

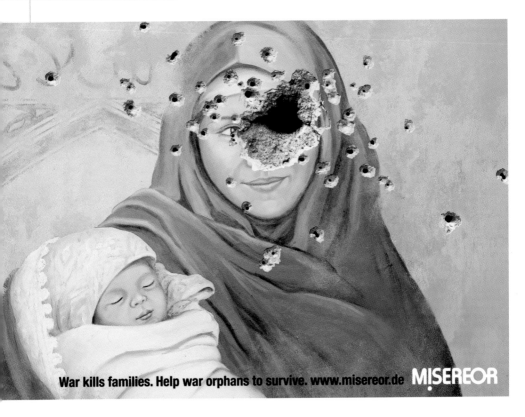

War kills families. Help war orphans to survive. www.misereor.de **MISEREOR**

MISEREOR: "WAR ORPHANS"

Agency: Kolle Rebbe, Hamburg
www.kolle-rebbe.de
Marketing manager: Georg Larscheid
Illustration: Eva Salzmann
Art director: Maik Beimdieck, Jens Lausenmeier
Copywriter: Elena Bartrina, Manns
Client: Bischöfliches Hilfswerk Misereor E.V.

Vileda: "For extra grip"

Agency: FP7 Doha
www.fp7.com
Art director: Maged Nassar
Creative director: Fadi Yaish
Photographer: Garrigosa Studio
Postproduction: Garrigosa Studio
Copywriter: Mohamed Diaa
Client: Vileda

Basic instinct

Basic instinct

Basic instinct

PEDRAS SALGADAS: "BASIC INSTINCT"

Agency: Bassat Ogilvy Barcelona
www.ogilvy.es
Art director: Francesc Talamino
Creative director: Jaume Monés
Photographer: Garrigosa Studio
Client: Pedras Salgadas water

Little Miss Sexual Slave woke once again in a very strange place.
An angry man shouted at her for forgetting to do her chores.
After she had finished cooking, cleaning and washing
clothes, she went to her daily lessons.
Little Miss Sexual Slave learned so many things that day.
Like stopping herself from crying and shooting a gun
that she could barely carry.
Later, she even learned how to serve male combatants
in whichever way they desired.

More than 300 000 children are forced to fight in armies
and militias around the world. Many girl soldiers are
expected to provide sexual services as well as go into battle.
Visit www.amnesty.org.za and lay the foundation for a
global ban on the use of children as soldiers.

006 561 NPO

AMNESTY INTERNATIONAL

Agency: The Jupiter Drawing Room, South Africa
www.jupiter.co.za
Advertising campaign: Miss Sexual Slave, Mr Genocide, Mr Mutilate
Art director: Neil Gardner
Creative director: Ross Chowles
Copywriter: PJ Kingsley
Client: Amnesty International

Little Mr Genocide was glad to see the sunshine again.
He didn't like those three weeks in the dark cell.
He was treated to a bowl of rice and then some cocaine and
marijuana. This was to help him be braver when he had to burn
houses with families locked inside or to carry
the severed heads of enemy soldiers.
One day, he refused to continue his training because it was
very hard and he was very tired. So he was beaten to death
in front of thirty other children and his body was thrown into the bushes.

More than 300 000 children are forced to fight in
armies and militias around the world. Some are as young as five.
Visit www.amnesty.org.za and lay the foundation
for a global ban on the use of children as soldiers.

Little Mr Mutilate woke up to a still breeze and a light blue sky.
He rubbed his big eyes and blinked a few times.
He had dreamed that he was taken from his bed in the night.
His dream had come true.
Next to him, a little boy cried.
Later, the crying boy would refuse to fight in a war
that he did not understand.
Little Mr Mutilate would be forced at
gunpoint to kill the boy with a machete.

More than 300 000 children under the age of 18 are fighting
in conflicts around the world. Hundreds of thousands more are
members of armed forces who could be sent into combat at any time.
Visit www.amnesty.org.za and lay the foundation for a
global ban on the use of children as soldiers.

TMB: "Large Films don't fit in here"

Agency: Bassat Ogilvy, Barcelona
www.ogilvy.es
Art director: Francesc Talamino
Creative director: Francesc Talamino
Photographer: Garrigosa Studio
Postproduction: Garrigosa Studio
Copywriter: Nacho Magro
Client: TMB (Transports metropolitans de Barcelona)

FRIENDS OF CANCER PATIENTS

Agency: Saatchi & Saatchi, Netherlands
www.saatchi.com
Advertising campaign: F-word, Stairway, 12.4 Seconds
Creative director: Magnus Olsson
Copywriter: Avinash Sampath
Art director: Tim Bishop
Illustrator: Gregory Ferrand
Retoucher: Jeroen Wartenbergh
Client: Friends of cancer patients

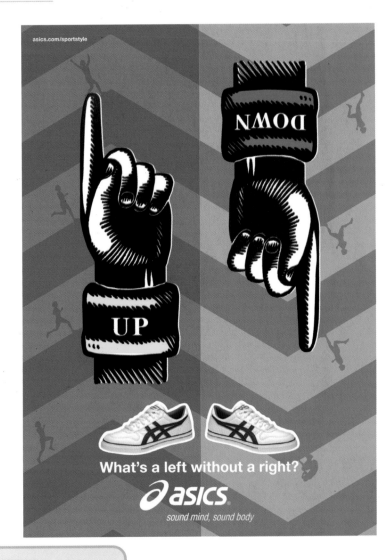

ASICS:
"LEFT AND RIGHT"

Agency: Amsterdam Worldwide
www.amsterdamworldwide.com
Executive creative director: Richard Gorodecky
Creative director: Andrew Watson
Client: ASICS SportStyle

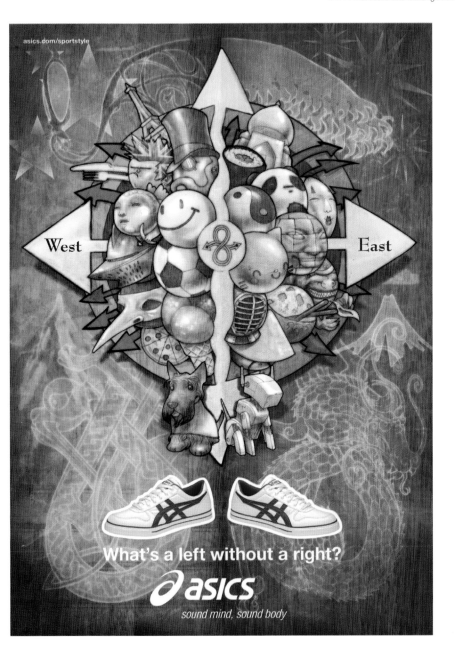

Yamaha: "Deep passion"

Agency: 1861 United Milan
www.1861united.com
Art director: Giorgio Cignoni
Creative director: Giorgio Cignoni
Photographer: Garrigosa Studio
Client: Yamaha Marine Motor

What runs through your veins
runs better without cholesterol.

Eating Cheerios for six weeks
can reduce cholesterol by 4%.

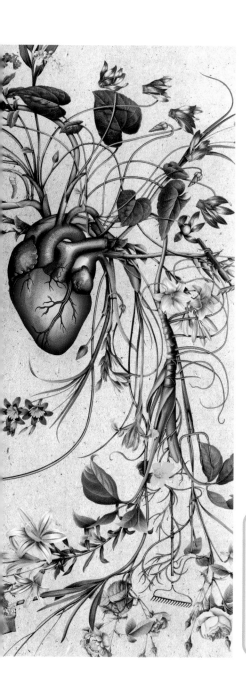

CHEERIOS

Agency: Saatchi & Saatchi New York
www.saatchi.com
Advertising campaign: Gardening, Rock & Roll
Copywriter: Icaro Doria
Illustrator: Mario Wagner, Dave Wheeler, Erin Petson
Clip art: Jaclyn Rink, Yab Apostolides, Aaron Padin
Typography: Hamish Mcarthur, Jaclyn Rink
Client: Cheerios

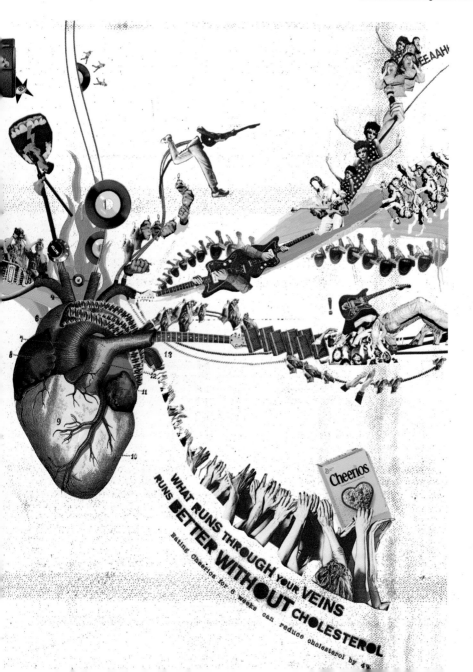

El moment en que una persona que necessita ajuda
es troba amb una persona que necessita ajudar.

Centre
per a
la Pau

Creu Roja

CRUZ ROJA

Agency: Villarrosàs
www.villarrosas.com
Advertising campaign: Centre per la Pau - Creu Roja
Art director: Eider Suso, Cristina Martin
Creative director: Oriol Villar
Graphic: David Fernandez
Client: Cruz Roja

HONDA CIVIC TIERRA

Agency: Villarrosàs
Art director: Enric Soldevila
Creative director: Oriol Villar, Fernando Codina
Graphic: Brosmind
Client: Honda

DOSE.CA

Agency: Rethink Communications, Vancouver
www.rethinkcommunications.com
Advertising campaign: Paris, Tom, Amy
Art director: Lisa Lebedovich
Writer: Rob Tarry
Creative director: Ian Grais, Chris Staples
Print producer: Jim Leith
Photographer: Hans Sipma
Studio artist: Jonathon Cesar, Richard Parkes, Justin Renvoize, Rory O'Sullivan (Type)
Gum art Paris: Jason Kronewald
Crochet art Amy: Animals in Yarn
Lego art Tom: Laura Munger
Client: Dose.ca

WATCH THEM FORM.
WATCH THEM UNRAVEL.

Estrella Levante

Agency: Villarrosàs
www.villarrosas.com
Advertising campaign: Concurso de Maquetas
Art director: Dani Zomeño
Creative director: Claudio Letelier, Oriol Villar
Graphic: Alex Trochut
Client: Estrella Levante

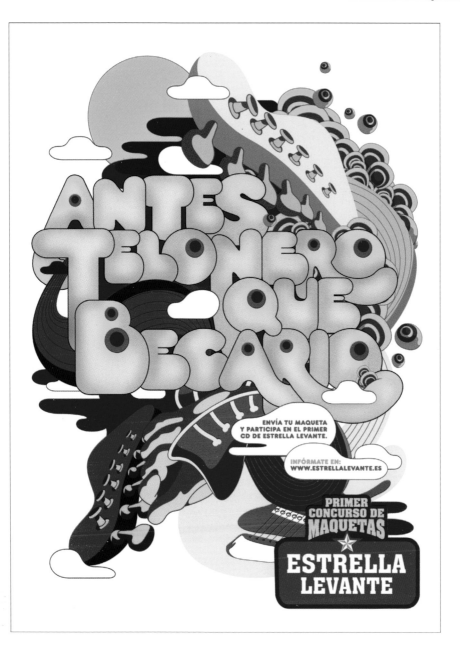

MANGO

Agency: Grupo Bassat Ogilvy
www.ogilvy.es
Art director: Francesc Talamino
Creative director: Francesc Talamino, Isa Sanchez
Photographer: Garrigosa Studio
Copywriter: Isa Sanchez
Client: Mango

SOS MATA ATLANTICA: "BUREAUCRACY KILLS NATURE"

Agency: F/Nazca Saatchi & Saatchi, Brazil
www.saatchi.com
Creative director: Fabio Fernandes, Eduardo Lima
Art director: Marco Monteiro
Writer: André Kassu
Account director: Tatiana Moliterno
Illustrator: Marco Monteiro
Client: SOS Mata Atlantica

UNUSUAL ADVERTISING